Josie Marie

From God, through Daisy

A THIRTY-DAY DEVOTIONAL TO GROW
YOUR AWARENESS OF GOD'S PRESENCE
IN SIMPLE, EVERYDAY MOMENTS

JOSIE MARIE

WESTBOW
P R E S S®
A DIVISION OF THOMAS NELSON
& ZONDERVAN

WestBow Press books may be ordered through booksellers or by contacting:

WestBow Press
A Division of Thomas Nelson & Zondervan
1663 Liberty Drive
Bloomington, IN 47403
www.westbowpress.com
844-714-3454

ISBN: 978-1-6642-9122-5 (sc)
ISBN: 978-1-6642-9124-9 (hc)
ISBN: 978-1-6642-9123-2 (e)

Library of Congress Control Number: 2023901740

Print information available on the last page.

WestBow Press rev. date: 02/23/2023

For my Lord and Savior, Jesus Christ,
the true author of this book,
I am so grateful for your presence in my
life, and I marvel at the way you work.

And my husband,
my earthly soulmate. Thank you for your
constant love and encouragement.
You make everything better, and I love
doing life with you. I love you IJHN!

And our girls,
whose insistence caused such a blessing
to be brought into our lives. You are
our joy, and we love you MTA!

Lastly, for my sister Robin,
thank you for your assistance and
support, not only with this project
but throughout my life. I love you!

Contents

Introduction

Welcome

HELLO, READER. I AM SO glad you picked up this book. Was it the title that caused you to do so? It does make one wonder what is contained within. Or perhaps it was that adorable face on the cover? Who could blame you if it were the latter? That face belongs to our sweet poodle, Daisy. Or as I like to call her (much to my husband's exasperation), "my sweet baby girl Daisy." But before I talk about Daisy and how this book came to be, I need to take you back to our first family dog, Buddy.

Buddy was a standard poodle who grew up alongside our two daughters. He looked a lot like Daisy but slightly blonder and bigger. I guess we have a thing for golden-colored poodles! They are an amazing family pet—loving, great with kids, hypoallergenic, and easy to train. Buddy was so sweet, obedient, and playful, with a contented, calm spirit. He was just the best dog a family could have. Sadly, a liver disease caused him to lose weight and get weak. However, we were blessed to have had twelve years with him. In the end, God was faithful to answer our family prayers that Buddy would pass quickly, at home, and surrounded by his family. He passed within fifteen minutes on our kitchen floor with our oldest daughter, my husband, and myself surrounding him, while we Face-timed our youngest daughter who was away at college. We don't know who it was more difficult for, those holding Buddy or our youngest who had to watch on her screen. Either way, the experience was heartbreaking. I know many of you can relate.

Needless to say, we were never getting another dog. I mean, how could we top Buddy? Who would ever want to go through that heartbreak again? Not me. I was done. So happy to have had Buddy, but he was enough for me. My husband agreed. The girls? Well, not so much. One year after Buddy died, they started dropping hints about wanting another dog. "No way," was our response. Time passed. Occasionally other comments were made. "When you get your own place, you can have as many dogs as you like," was our response. (How many of you can hear yourself saying that?) Winter 2020 came around, and we were all cooped up in the house due to COVID, and the comments surfaced again … but this time my walls started tumbling. I started to think how nice it might be to have another dog around, but a small dog this time, one that is easier to care for, easier to pick up after, easier to transport, etc. The girls and I started looking online. Big mistake! All hesitation vanished upon looking at those adorable, tiny faces! We waited for the perfect moment to ask Daddy. "No way," once again. Then, one day out of the blue, he came downstairs and said, "We can get a dog."

What? What happened? He proceeded to explain that while praying he felt God say, "Life is short; get the girls a dog." "Yes, Sir!" was his response, and we didn't have to be told twice. After much searching, we found Daisy at the same breeder from whom we received Buddy.

Now Daisy is technically a standard poodle also, but she is part of a subgroup of standards called moyen poodles. They are a smaller standard, roughly around thirty to forty pounds. We picked the runt of the litter hoping she would stay small, as we didn't want another big dog. Daisy was five pounds when we took her home. See the picture? Isn't she just the cutest? But she didn't stay so small, which leads me into our first devotional.

I hope that you will reread these daily thoughts often and be reminded of God's presence in everyday moments. Curl up in a quiet spot and enjoy the pages to follow as we hear from God, through our wonderful new blessing, Daisy. God bless you!

Day 1

Trust in God's Sovereign Knowledge

HAVE YOU EVER HAD PRAYERS answered in ways other than what you were expecting? All the time, right? It is a lifelong desire for God to line my will up with His. In the Gospel of John, chapter 14, verse 13, Jesus states: "And I will do whatever you ask in My name, so that the Son may bring glory to the Father." These words bring me great comfort because I know that whatever I ask for, if it's in line with the Father's will (1 John 5:14–15), then it will be done. If it's not, then it wasn't the Father's will, and who can argue with that, right? Well, the journey of getting Daisy was an opportunity for my family and me to exercise such trust.

We were so excited to get a new puppy. We covered our search in prayer, inviting God into every detail—what type of dog, what color, what size, what gender, and so forth. We prayed the puppy would be super cuddly, calm, and, as already mentioned, small. We had downsized to a condo a couple of years prior, so we knew we didn't have the space for a large dog (smaller rooms, no fenced-in yard, etc.). The breeder we received our first dog, Buddy, from only raised moyen and standard poodles, both bigger than we desired. But we went to visit her new puppy litter "just to see." While there, we felt God leading us toward our now Daisy. She was the smallest of the litter, and we prayed she would stay small! And for the first month, she did. Her five-pound frame was so adorable and easy to control. But it didn't take long before we were wondering where our little puppy went. Suddenly, we couldn't wash her in the sink anymore, the living room seemed half its already small size, and her bark sounded like a bullhorn. And her energy! So much energy! Where did our sleepy, calm, easily carried pup go?

Daisy is now twenty-six months old. She is forty-one pounds, strong as an ox, feisty, and has endless energy. It makes me laugh just writing about it. These past two years have been so much fun with her. Because of her size, her strength, and her energy, we are outside *a lot*. And no fenced yard means one or more of us is outside with her. We walk, run, go to the park or to the beach, hike—whatever it takes to give Daisy exercise and drain that poodle energy. I don't believe we would do this to the same extent if she were the ten-pound pup we desired. You see, what I think we really wanted was a living stuffed animal. Stick with me here. We did indeed want a new puppy because we missed Buddy and the joy he'd brought to our daily life. However, we wanted a tiny pup, one that we could carry around, who would sit still on our laps, who would adjust to our schedule, who would bring us joy and comfort but who wouldn't be too disruptive. The total opposite of Daisy! She is high maintenance from sunup to sundown. But we wouldn't want it any other way. We totally adore her. Yes, God knew what we needed versus what we wanted. With our girls grown and away or working full-time, Daisy has been a unifying factor for us, causing us to slow down some, visit frequently, get outside more, and take walks together, laughing at Daisy's antics the entire time. It's all part of God's will for me and my family. God knows best.

Sometimes we get disappointed with prayer. Either we feel silence or things turn out differently than we had hoped. We know from scripture that God answers our prayers even before we finish speaking (Daniel 9:20–23). We don't always receive the answer we are looking for, but when we lift our hearts' desires up to Him, we can rest in His faithfulness to work out everything in conformity with His perfect will, whether a major life decision or simply the addition of a new family pet. His answer is good not only for us but for all involved.

Thank You, heavenly Father, that You are sovereign.
You know what we need, and Your plans for
us are good. Help us grow in surrendering all
things to You and in trusting that You will work
everything out according to Your perfect will.
In Jesus's Name, we pray, *amen.*

Key scriptures:
Isaiah 65:24
Proverbs 16:9
Ephesians 1:11
Deuteronomy 32:3–4

Day 2

Rest in God's Embrace

REMEMBER WHEN I MENTIONED OUR desire for our new pup to be calm and cuddly? Well, here is another example of God speaking to us through Daisy in unexpected ways: our feisty, energetic, big dog is also our sweet, cuddly lapdog. I know it seems contradictory, but it's true. One minute she can be wrestling with you ferociously, and the next she is climbing up onto your chair to rest against your body. And sometimes against your body isn't enough; she will drape herself over your legs and fall asleep, so happy to be rubbed and to know you are close. God gave us a cuddler. We just didn't expect our legs to fall asleep in the process!

Now, there's no one Daisy loves to wrestle with more than my husband, and they play hard. I often must look away because I can't stand to watch.

"Don't hurt her," I say, because someone usually gets hurt, right, moms?

My husband responds, "I'm trying to avoid her hurting me."

And he means it. Daisy sounds like she's ripping him limb from limb. She just loves it, and bonus: it really drains that energy we talked about! But sometimes Daisy just gets too worked up, and the fun needs to stop. "All done" is her command to stop all current play. She obeys well, but one night she just wasn't stopping. She wanted to play and didn't care that my husband felt differently. He looked at me as if to say, "Can you make her stop, please?"

Our oldest daughter witnessed the exchange and commented, "No one calms her like you do, Mom."

My husband sweetly added, "That's because Daisy sees her as her mamma."

Of course that made me feel great, and it's true. I do not work outside the house, so Daisy and I spend all day, all night together. I usually take her on errands, too, as I hate to crate her. Not good, I know; I'm working on improving this. But my husband's comment is accurate; they are Daisy's playmates, and I am her pack leader. So, I scooped up my sweet baby girl Daisy and placed her on my lap. She tested my restraint, but when she realized that I wasn't letting go, she softened into my hold and quickly fell asleep lying entirely on my body, her soft fluffy head resting on my shoulder. My forty-one-pound cuddler. So precious.

In that quiet moment I reflected on God's presence and how He can quiet and calm me like no other. I have a wonderful husband, two close daughters, and other family and friends, all of whom I thank God for. But they are my playmates compared to my one and only pack leader, Jesus. I smiled at this and gave Daisy a gentle squeeze, knowing in my heart that just as I needed to step in and calm her, Jesus does that for me when I'm all worked up, worried, stressed, saddened, fearful, and so on. He holds me tight and comforts me with His loving embrace.

Do you need comfort today? Are you going through something that's got you all worked up? Jesus is close. He promises to never leave us or forsakes us (Deuteronomy 31:6). No matter how we are feeling or what we are experiencing, we can always curl up and cuddle with God, whose lap is always big enough and whose arms are always wide enough. Let us rest in His embrace today.

Praise You, Father, for Your presence that never
leaves us. You are always right there to step
in and return us to a place of calm. Train us,
please, to make You our first response, to cuddle
up with You and receive Your comfort.
In Jesus's Name, *amen.*

Key scriptures:
Deuteronomy 33:27
Psalm 18:6
Psalm 94:19
Psalm 91:1
Matthew 11:28

Day 3

Allow God's Protective Love

AS I SHARED EARLIER, WHEN we first brought Daisy home, she weighed all of five pounds. I would bring her to visit my parents, who fell in love with her instantly. In the beginning, I held her on my lap while I drove, and she almost always fell asleep to the comfort of my touch and the humming of the drive. I realized the danger this practice held for both of us. (Talk about a distraction!) So we purchased a doggie "car seat" that held Daisy's small frame, anchoring our new baby in safety. However, she was not as thrilled as we were about this option. Although secured in her seat, she repeatedly tried to climb out of the bucket and onto my lap. Whining constantly, she would stretch out her paws to try and reach me, working herself into quite a tizzy as she tangled herself up in the seat strap. This was more distracting than her sleeping on my lap! But I held firm, knowing this new practice would keep her safe and allow me to focus on the road. I knew she would adjust, and this means of travel would become her new normal. She didn't understand why she couldn't crawl up close and be held. She didn't see the danger it posed. But I did, and safety needed to come first.

I'm sure every one of us can think of a time when something happened that we didn't understand or approve of. Or maybe it's something that didn't happen instead. And it doesn't necessarily have to be a big life moment. Small, everyday displeasures can create quite a lot of frustration. Maybe plans with friends fell through at the last minute, creating disappointment. Perhaps a minor sickness prevented a family vacation. Ever get stuck in traffic that caused late arrival to your next destination? Just like Daisy didn't understand why she could no longer lie in my lap during drive time, we don't always understand the whys of everyday events. Perhaps God is keeping us, or someone else, safe from an unwanted accident. Maybe plans fall through so we will be available later in the day to help a friend in need. Changes in our schedule could allow our paths to cross with someone who needs to hear the gospel. We don't always know, but we can trust God's plan. His ways are higher than our ways. He sees all and knows all and, yes, He protects us from what we don't know and from what we can't see, because He loves us. When we invite Him into our day, we can trust Him with what comes and with what is held back, knowing He is guiding our path. His plan is perfect. His timing is perfect. He is perfect. Who better to go before us!

Let's play a game, shall we? The next time we find ourselves getting all tangled and into a tizzy because of something we don't understand, let's pause and try to think of as many reasons as we can as to why God would allow or prevent the situation at hand. At first, just try to think of one reason. When you come up with one, think of another, and so on. Keep devising reasons until you find yourself calm and resting in the truths above. Until you can surrender to His plan, His timing, His protective love.

Father God, Your Word tells us that Your ways
are higher than our ways, and Your thoughts are

higher than our thoughts. Praise You for this! We know You sit enthroned above the circle of the earth, and Your eyes watch over us. Thank You for protecting us from what we don't even know is around. Thank You for guiding us through day-to-day frustrations that we would rather not face. Increase our trust in You and our surrender of daily moments to You. In Jesus's Name, *amen.*

Key scriptures:
Isaiah 40:22, 55:8–9
Psalm 66:7
Psalm 18:30
Psalm 91:11–12
Proverbs 3:5–6

Day 4

Accept God's Offer of Prayer

ONE OF MY FAVORITE MOMENTS of the day with Daisy is our early morning "Bible Time." When we first awake, the house bustles with family members getting ready for work, getting Daisy outside for her morning routine, making tea, etc. But when these family members leave, and others remain asleep, complete silence settles. This is "Bible Time." Daisy and I curl up on our living room loveseat, morning sunshine streams through the curtains, and I take a deep breath knowing how precious this intimate time with my Lord is. This routine is a direct answer to prayer. You see, the Lord taught me a long time ago the truth in His Word regarding praying on all occasions with all kinds of prayers and requests (Ephesians 6:18). So when Daisy was young and full of energy in the morning, and my Bible reading time was threatened, I started asking God to give Daisy a spirit of calm and protect my quiet time with Him. Then, I was mindful to create a routine that led up to "Bible Time," including when we began, where we sat, and how I phrased "Bible Time." God has been faithful. He blessed this consistent routine and helped my sweet puppy learn that when I announce "Bible Time," she needs to settle down and lie quietly aside of me. I am so thankful, and she's such a good girl. She lies there until she hears me stop talking, and my Bible closes. Sensing I am finished, she will lift her head and stare at me, waiting for the announcement of her favorite moment of the day: "Wanna go for a walk?" With tail wagging exuberantly, she rushes off the loveseat and straight to the front door. Yup! She's ready!

The invitation to commune with our heavenly Father anytime and about anything is such a gift. On day 1, I mentioned John 14:13 where Jesus states: "And I will do whatever you ask in My name, so that the Son may bring glory to the Father." This verse grows my confidence in prayer. However, many times still exist where I forget to lift a matter before the One who knows all things. I make plans without laying them at His feet; I move forward with a decision without consulting His wisdom, and I get caught up in stress, forgetting to surrender my issue to Him so I may receive His peace. Lately, I have been convicted as I feel His Holy Spirit's gentle reminder that He desires to be part of everything I do. Can you relate? As we recall today's events, let's think of plans, decisions, etc. where we relied on our own wisdom, our own strength, our own understanding, or our own desires instead of consulting our Father and relying on Him. Yes, God does give us strong minds to act with wisdom and intelligence. But He still desires us to come to Him, and it honors Him when we do. If we fall short in this area, don't worry, there is no condemnation in Christ Jesus (Romans 8:1). We can pray for God to turn us from self-reliance and grow us in the knowledge of how much He desires to be involved in our day to day. Nothing is too big or too small. He cares about it all because He cares about us.

Do you feel awkward praying about silly, simple things with the Creator of the universe? But this is exactly what prayer is— just simple conversation with God. Maybe it would help if you picture Him either on His throne or physically sitting next to you. Maybe you could journal your prayers and then read them back to the Lord. Whatever will help you develop comfort, do it. Maybe you're comfortable talking with God but life is full of distractions that get in the way of remembering to include Him. We can all relate for sure. I have often left sticky notes in various places such as the fridge or on my phone with scripture verses on them to help train a prayer habit. Perhaps this will help you? Or maybe wearing a special bracelet or placing a small prayer book in your lunch box will be the aide you need to invite God into the moments of your day. Whatever will help, do it. We need to be intentional about training to be prayer minded. And we also need to be consistent with the tools we use and the routines we create so they become solid daily habits.

And yes, we should always have a heart of reverence as we enter God's presence, but we must also remember that in addition to being Creator of the universe, He is also our loving Daddy. He is intimate, tender, and compassionate, and He invites us to draw near. Incredible, right?! The Almighty Creator invites us to talk with Him anytime, anywhere, and about anything. Let's take Him up on that. Let's lay everything at His feet—cares, struggles, joys, desires, daily schedules—everything! And as 1 John 5:14–15 says, we can trust that His will *will* be done because we have invited Him in. What peace!

Let's pray together for God to grow our love and practice of prayer:

Father above, we thank You for the gift of prayer
and for Your desire for us to come to You with

all things. Your grace toward us is overwhelming. Please protect us from the busyness of life that gets in the way. Guard our quiet times with You and grow our love of prayer throughout our days. Teach us how to pray and enter Your presence. In Jesus's Name, *amen.*

Key scriptures:
James 4:8
Psalm 145:18
Matthew 6:9–13
Colossians 4:2
Psalm 66:20

Day 5

Desire God's Closeness

ON DAY 2, I MENTIONED how Daisy loves to be held nice and close. Really, she just loves to be touched in any way. She'll walk in between your legs and stand there waiting for you to massage her lower back and hind legs. She loves a face rub, and if you approach her while she is lying still, a rare moment for sure, she will sense your presence and roll onto her back to welcome a belly rub. Touch is definitely one of her love languages! One day during "Bible Time" she was lying by my side with her face and front paws resting on my right thigh. After several moments, her front paw reached out and grabbed hold of my left leg. With extended claws she proceeded to pull and wiggle until her chest rested on my lap. She settled in for a few moments until both front paws pulled and wiggled some more, positioning herself on and down the entire length of my two legs. I remember watching her and saying in my head, "Can you get any closer, sweet girl?" The overwhelming thought that came next echoed, "Do I desire to get closer and closer to You, Lord?"

I pray that question serves as our encouragement today. It is essential for Christians to draw near to Jesus every day, even every moment within the day, as we discussed yesterday. As we learn to pray to Him on all occasions with all kinds of prayers and requests (Ephesians 6:18), our closeness with Him will naturally strengthen. But the question for today is, "Do we *desire* to get closer?" If your response is a resounding yes, then keep pressing on, drawing near through prayer, the Word, in worship, with eyes to see and ears to hear. He will honor your desire.

But maybe some of us struggle with this desire. Maybe getting closer to God means we might have to address some things we would rather keep buried. Maybe we would have to make some changes in our daily practices, give up time and/or attention from other things. Maybe we just don't know what getting closer looks like. One scripture I just love states: "I consider everything a loss compared to the surpassing greatness of knowing Christ Jesus my Lord" (Philippians 3:8). This verse puts everything is perspective for me. He is worthy of our full desire. If we struggle with desiring a closer relationship with Jesus, let us follow the steps below and have our hearts open to His work within us. He will always provide help with whatever needs attention. He will honor your honesty.

1. Let us first *repent* over our hesitations, fears, doubts, worldly distractions, etc. Pray Psalm 139:23–24 and sit with God on it, allowing His Holy Spirit to reveal whatever is preventing a desire to grow closer to Him. He knows our hearts and minds (Psalm 94:11, Luke 16:15).

2. Next, let us *pray* for God to grow this desire for His nearness.

3. Be faithful to *read* the Word every day. It is God's love letter and will cause us to discover His character. Before you read, pray for wisdom and revelation through His Holy Spirit so you may know Him better (Ephesians 1:17).

4. *Memorize* key scriptures that will remind you throughout the day of His presence and His great love for you. Some suggestions are John 3:16 and Romans 8:37–39.

5. Take steps for *action*. Drawing near does not always involve quiet alone time. We also draw near to Him as we put into practice our knowledge of what pleases Him by doing likewise. This gives us an opportunity to reflect our Savior to those around us. God has work for us to do while here on this earth—work that involves sharing who He is and all that Jesus has done for us, so that others too may be saved to eternal life. We must share the gospel of Christ in word and in deed. As we cooperate with God in this all-important mission, we see Him work wonders through us. This strengthens our faith, and our hunger for Him will grow even more.

Loving Father, You are with us this day, and we thank You. Help us have ears to hear Your Holy Spirit's voice and quiet our hearts and minds so we may draw near. Grow our desire to know You better and our joy in reflecting You to the world. In Jesus's holy Name, *amen*.

Key scriptures:
Psalm 42:1–2
James 4:8
Psalm 73:25
John 6:35

Day 6

Acknowledge God's Presence

DAISY AND I WALK EVERY day, but her favorite thing is to run off leash. Who can blame her? And she needs to run as much as we need her to! We have a large field behind our condo unit that we like to visit. Daisy knows when we walk in the field's direction and pulls on her leash with great anticipation. When I remove her leash and wave my hand for her to run, she takes off! She's so happy, running for the sake of running. Without the constraint of the leash, she can explore and be free. I just smile watching her have so much fun being a dog. Truthfully, I'm saying to myself, "Keep running, sweet girl, get nice and tired for Mamma."

What's so sweet is that as Daisy is flying free, she repeatedly stops and looks around for me. She's been so distracted by every sight, sound, and smell that she doesn't realize how far she's drifted. She, of course, doesn't know that I am watching her the entire time ensuring that she doesn't go too far and that she is safe. But I love to see her looking for me, and when she does, she comes sprinting back as if to say, "Did you see me, Mom?" Then, with renewed confidence that I am close, she takes off again.

Once when I was watching her, I felt God relating the moment to His presence with us and how He is always there—watching over us, protecting us from harm, guiding us through life, and preventing us from going too far. I was reminded that we can look to him constantly and get confirmation of His love and His presence through everyday moments. His presence gives us confidence to keep doing whatever it is He has called us to do, and when we turn to Him, he is always there. What a gift!

Sometimes the busyness of life can be quite distracting. We can be off running free, doing our own thing. We forget that God is with us and longs to be part of whatever we are doing. We are never alone, and therefore never without direction, wisdom, hope, comfort, companionship, or love. For God is all these things and more, and He is always ready to fill us with what we need.

Do we turn to God to receive assurance of His presence? Just like Daisy would look around for me to ensure that I was close, are we looking for God in our everyday moments? He is all around us, always. We can get confirmation of God's nearness as we look for Him in our family interactions, in the encouragement of a friend, in the lyrics of our favorite song, in the beauty of a sunset or a soaring hawk. He is present each time we open His Word, each time we turn to Him in prayer, and in each daily moment He blesses us with—we can look for Him and say "hello" to acknowledge His nearness.

Heavenly Father, we thank You for Your never-ending presence. Thank You for allowing us to know You. Help us to look for You, Lord, and to have eyes to see. Grow our confidence that You are always there as we draw close to You in prayer, in Your Word, and in every daily moment. In Jesus's Name, *amen.*

Key scriptures:
Psalm 139:7–8
Psalm 121
John 14:16–17a
Matthew 28:20b

Day 7

Discover God's Voice

NOT ONLY DOES DAISY GET great exercise and fresh air while enjoying her off leash freedom of the field behind our condo, but our time there also serves to instill obedience in our adventurous, feisty little (or not so little) Daisy. Win, win! I knew when we decided to welcome a new puppy into our family that I would start training immediately. Our first dog, Buddy, was wonderfully obedient, most of the time. I say this with great love for him, and I still chuckle at how he would take off at the sight of anything with legs ... dog, cat, bunny, frog, it didn't matter. If it moved, he wanted to play with it. And it did not matter how many times we would call him. We would even shake his treat container while yelling, "Come." But all our attempts fell on deaf ears when he was in pursuit of a furry friend, and he had an undivided focus. This used to annoy me beyond words. We spent so much money and time in training him, and he acted as if he never heard our commands before.

Well, not with Daisy, I vowed. I started using training commands right away, especially "come" even when I knew she was too young to really understand. I coupled praise with treats. Oh yes, many treats! From the very beginning I wanted her to know that coming to Mamma meant getting good stuff. I also shower her obedience with my best high-pitched voice, which my husband just loves to hear!

The big open field, when Daisy is running free and exploring, allows great opportunities for me to instill this "come" response. I will purposely walk away from her only to call "come" at random times. Whether near or far, I want her to recognize my voice. One day, instead of saying "come," I made a clicking noise, almost like a kissing sound, and kept doing it until she came. I kept training her with this noise, loving its uniqueness to me. I encouraged my husband and daughters to also find their own unique sound for Daisy. These sounds have become interchangeable with "come," and they work just as well at achieving the goal—when we call her, we want her to drop everything and come. High expectation we know, especially when competing with other furry friends.

In the Gospel of John, chapter 10, Jesus refers to Himself as our Good Shepherd. He describes how His sheep know His voice and they listen to Him. When I'm in the field training Daisy, I think of this teaching from my Lord. The title *Lord* means *Master*. As Daisy's pack leader, I am her master, the authority figure in her life. So it is important to me that she knows my voice, my clicks, my claps, even the changes in my facial expressions.

It is exponentially more vital for us Christians to know our Savior's voice. Praise God for the Bible, what a treasure! There are a lot of competing voices in our day-to-day walk, but it is within the pages of scripture that we discover the distinction of Jesus's voice. It grows us to know His character, what pleases Him, and His deep truths that bring life. Reading His Word, sitting with Him in prayer, enjoying Christian fellowship. These all train us to know Jesus and His voice. In Matthew 11:29, Jesus says: "Take my yoke upon you and *learn from me*, for I am gentle and humble in heart, and you will find rest for your souls" (italics mine). There is no greater responsibility for Christ followers. We learn from Him by reading His Word and discovering His character, His commands, and His voice above all others, even our own. It helps us know truth in a world of lies and deception. It empowers us to follow our Master, as His voice clearly marks the way.

As brothers and sisters in Christ, let us make a pact to read the Bible every day; it is vital to our spiritual maturity. It is vital so we can know our Master's voice and respond as He would. There are so many things in a day to vie for our attention, but let us set aside time to draw close to our Master so that we may learn from Him, and as a result, echo His voice to a world in need.

> Father, thank You for giving us Your Word, a light
> unto our path. We ask that You would–fine tune
> our ears to Jesus's voice, helping us know His ways
> so that we may follow His example. We pray in
> the Name of our Lord, our Master, Jesus, *amen*.

Key scriptures:
Psalm 119:105
Psalm 32:8
Isaiah 30:21

Day 8

Respond to God's Voice

OFF LEASH. TWO WONDERFUL WORDS for Daisy. And usually I agree. However, there are times when I want the comfort and security of the leash. Sometimes it is necessary for Daisy's safety; other times it's just me wanting to know she's close and secure. As previously mentioned, our first dog, Buddy, had a history of seeing any open door and escaping through it to chase after whatever furry friend appeared in his view. So although I enjoy taking Daisy to an open field where she can run and explore, I often pray for God to keep her safe as I detach leash from collar. Despite my hesitation, I do know these periods of unbound freedom are so good for her exercise and obedience. We discussed yesterday how these open field days are a great time to train Daisy to know my voice and my ways. But it's not enough for her to just know my voice; I want her to respond! Even if four other things are competing for her attention, if I call, I want her to come running. What's the point of training otherwise, right?

Am I responding to my Master? Are you? Just like Daisy needs to respond to me, we need to respond to our Master, Jesus, when He calls. Sometimes God lets us run and explore as well. Perhaps we won't know God's direction until we do so. Other times God allows the exploration to test obedience. Will we come running back to His commands amid a vast and tempting world? Will we listen to the Holy Spirit and allow Jesus's voice to prevail? Will we respond and put all our training into practice?

God is always right there with us, even if we stay too long in an open field and don't return right away. He could make us respond. But out of love, He gives us free will, which means we get to choose to respond or not. His will for us is good, and when we respond to His voice and stand for His ways, His will can be accomplished in our lives. He also grows us in strength to continue to respond and deepens our relationship with Him, which is far better than whatever distraction kept us from responding in the first place.

If we find ourselves not responding to Jesus's voice for any reason, it is always the right moment to turn in repentance and be filled with His love. He is always ready to receive us and our recommitment to follow His ways.

> Heavenly Father, we do desire to live in a way
> that pleases You so we pray You will strengthen
> us to obey and respond to Your calling. Show us
> areas of our lives where we are not responding as
> Jesus would and lead us back into the light of Your
> presence. Protect us from distractions and even
> our own desires. In Jesus's Name we pray, *amen.*

Key scriptures:
1 John 1:9
Colossians 2:6
James 1:22–25
John 14:21

Day 9

Look to God Always

HAVE ANY OF YOU JOINED a puppy training class? Oh, what fun! We had attended such a class with our previous dog, Buddy, which equipped us to train Daisy when we first welcomed her home. She knew most of the commands already, but we still signed her up for puppy "kindergarten" when she was old enough. We wanted the socialization aspect, as well as instilling obedience of the already known commands among the distraction of other people and dogs. Daisy loved class! She, of course, just wanted to play, but she did well and was very stimulated, which made her sleep like a baby when we got home. Total bonus!

One command the instructor taught was "look at me." She emphasized the importance of this command: If a dog turns its head and eyes away from its owner the animal gets all distracted by what's around it and loses obedience. Therefore, it helps to give the "look at me" command to get the dog's attention prior to giving another command. During the drive home from class, I was thinking of this teaching and how it rings so true to humans as well. Okay, I'll speak personally—how it rings true to me as well. Why is it so easy to take our eyes off God and His truths and focus on the distractions around us instead? Maybe it's because those distractions are so real, so tangible. And they are. Sickness is felt physically. Stress eats away at us mentally. Difficulty in relationships wears us down emotionally. The standards and treasures of this world distract us spiritually. And just like Peter, we begin to sink as we focus on these circumstances rather than on our life Instructor, Jesus (Matthew 14:22–33). Big or small, frequent or rare, as we go through life's challenges, Jesus invites us to look at Him so He can see us through. He promises to guide our path, but we must first look to Him so He can give us further instructions. He is faithful to meet our gaze with open arms and supply us with everything we need physically, mentally, emotionally, and spiritually.

Sometimes during difficult circumstances, words escape us. As we try to pray, distraction prevails as the current difficulty weighs heavy on our hearts and minds. We need not worry. God knows what we would say even before we say it. We can simply "look at Him" by acknowledging His presence. We can sit in silence trusting His Holy Spirit to pray for us (Romans 8:26). We can draw near by reading the Bible, relying on His words rather than ours. I also enjoy worship music during such times, letting the lyrics serve as my prayer. Whatever means we choose, God is honored by our drawing near and promises to gladly, without hesitation, meet us where we are.

> Father above, we thank You for Your invitation
> to look to You always and Your promise to
> supply our every need in Christ, Your Son.
> Strengthen us to keep our eyes on You above
> everything else and train us to turn and look

at You, rather than the circumstances around us. We praise You for Your faithfulness.

In Jesus's Name, *amen.*

Key scriptures:
2 Chronicles 20:12
Matthew 6:33
Philippians 4:19
2 Peter 1:3–4

Day 10

Move Forward with God

YESTERDAY'S DEVOTION ABOUT LOOKING TO Jesus for all things is the perfect segue to discuss moving forward in general. Which, of course, the Lord reminded me about during an average day encounter with my beloved Daisy.

We were out enjoying our morning walk, practicing Daisy's training commands as we strolled along. Don't want her forgetting those hard-earned obedience lessons! However, on that day, she just would not obey. She struggled with almost every command I gave and was just bopping around without a care in the world. Tugging on the leash, running in circles around me, jumping up trying to body slam me (I'm not kidding), all the while with a twinkle in her eyes that no doubt expressed, "Not today, Mom." I knew a break was needed, so we headed to her favorite field and played fetch. "Why won't she listen lately?" I asked myself as I threw her stick. "Why is she going backward in training?" I wished our daughter's friend, Will, was around. He and his family have been training seeing eye dogs for years. We call him the "Daisy Whisperer" because of his command over her excitable personality. I definitely could have used his help on that day. I was a bit frustrated as I contemplated starting over and patiently guiding her back to the commands that I was confident she knew.

However, as I watched her run, a smile crept onto my face. She was having so much fun. I don't know why some days she excels while other days pose much more of a challenge, but I felt God's reminder of His incredible patience with me as He gently reteaches me lessons I should be well past learning. "You're right, Father," I acknowledged as I confessed my own tendency to forget, forego, or simply fight against lessons I have learned from Him.

So often God's grace pours out of His Word, giving us reminders and encouragements to follow His ways. Daisy's disobedience provided an opportunity to self-examine my own walk with God and allow Him to reveal areas where I was not listening, partially or fully. Are there areas in your life that are causing you to move backward in your walk? Are there issues God is training you on, but the fruit of your life says, "not today, Lord?" Rest assured, when we pause and pray for God to reveal our disobedience, to any extent and in any area, He is faithful to shine His light into our darkness. When we repent, He is faithful to forgive (1 John 1:9). He is patient, even if it means He starts over and retrains us from the beginning. He loves a humble, trainable heart, so let us be quick to repent and ask for His help.

Almighty Father, You are so patient with the stubborn likes of us, and we give You all praise for Your unending love and goodness. Break down our rebellion and disobedience and create in us, Elohim (Creator God), a wholehearted devotion to You and Your ways. Give us soft hearts to be trained by Your

Word so that our lives would reflect Your light to all around us. In Jesus's mighty Name we pray, *amen.*

Key scriptures:
2 Corinthians 13:5
Psalm 139:23–24
Psalm 18:28
Psalm 25

Day 11

Fight for God's Glory

ON THE LAST NIGHT OF puppy training class, our instructor surprised all the participants with a night of fun "games" to test our dogs' obedience, such as musical chairs but with hula hoops instead of chairs where owners as well as dogs needed to be inside the ring when the music ended. Last pair outside the ring lost that round. It was fun and was a great way to test how in tune owner and dog had become. The last game played was a relay race. The owner needed to hold a plastic egg on a spoon with one hand while holding his or her dog's leash with the other. They then were instructed to walk around several cones without dropping the egg and with having their dog remain in "heel" before stopping at the finish line where doggie needed to sit without having been asked. Also fun!

Daisy and I had been training consistently during our daily walks, so we participated with confidence. We made it to the finals. This was it—do or die. Well, Daisy did great! We made it through without an egg drop or sway from "heel." We approached the finish line, and Daisy sat as soon as I stopped. Such a good girl. But although we finished first, we lost. We accidentally stopped just inches over the finish line, not *at* the finish line. Yes, it's true. But as the other owner received her first-place ribbon, I looked down at Daisy and loved on her. I was so proud of her.

She followed me wherever I went and obeyed every command. I didn't need to insist that we were first, and we didn't need the victory prize. I knew she won, and that was good enough for me.

As I stood there processing the news that we didn't officially win, my mind immediately recalled a biblical lesson on fighting the good fight (1 Timothy 6:11–12), taught by Beth Moore, a well-known Bible teacher. Let's take a minute to read this verse and refresh ourselves with its truth.

> But you, man of God, flee from all this, and pursue righteousness, godliness, faith, love, endurance and gentleness. Fight the good fight of the faith. Take hold of the eternal life to which you were called when you made your good confession in the presence of many witnesses.

I will never forget Beth's teaching on the above scripture, as it greatly grew my ability to rest in what God sees and in what He says, which is huge for someone like myself who has dealt with lifelong insecurities. Fighting the good fight means knowing what the good fight is: Our reflection of our Savior so that our lives point others to Him, bringing the Father glory. Even with an insignificant event like a doggie relay, this biblical truth remains. Each day we all encounter moments that invite us to fight. You're most likely recalling an event as you read this. Perhaps someone cut you off while driving? Or maybe you didn't get a promotion you deserved? A child tested your patience? Been teased because of how you look or dress? Someone dismissed your thoughts on a subject? In countless situations each day, we feel wronged or slighted.

Now, I'm not saying we should never stand up for ourselves or correct a wrong. There are times when we should, and we should do so with humility and grace so that our good fight honors God. But often the issues we fight are not of significance and only serve to escalate our temper and stress and diminish our Christian witness. Pride wins over as we push the fight for the sake of winning, proving ourselves right, or to rest in what man thinks of us. Biblical truths free us from the concern for man's opinion and allow us to rest in what God thinks of us. It fills us with strength to know that what God says and sees is enough.

> Sovereign Father, one day You will right every wrong. Until then, train us to recognize what is worth fighting for and fill us with peace to let everything else go. Please reveal any fight within us that does not bring You glory, and help us to rest in the knowledge that You see all and know all. In Jesus's Name, *amen.*

Key scriptures:
Romans 12:17–21
Proverbs 16:7
Colossians 3:23–25
Psalm 19:14
Colossians 2:10

Day 12

Obey God Joyfully

IN THE GOSPEL OF MATTHEW, chapter 21, verses 28–32, Jesus tells a story about two brothers who received a command from their father. The first son initially says no to the given command but eventually obeys and completes the assigned task. The second son says, "Yes, Father" right away, but never does what he was instructed to do. Jesus asked the surrounding crowd, "Which of the two did what his father wanted?" The crowd answered, "the first." They are correct, of course. I love this story because we have a daughter who often resembles the first son. We have chuckled over this many times, and she will now say no with a smile on her face because she knows we know she's going to do whatever is in question.

It seems she has passed on her hesitant obedience to her new rambunctious poodle. Now, with much patience and perseverance on our part, Daisy has become a wonderfully obedient dog. Mind you, if off leash with distractions around, this statement might not hold true. But overall, the training has paid off, and Daisy excels. However, much like the first son in Jesus's story, Daisy's obedience does not always come right away. Sometimes, she makes us work for it. During play time, Daisy can get all worked up with excitement. Before she breeches an energetic point of no return, we attempt to calm her by directing her to her coveted living room spot, "her" ottoman. She has now learned that this means fun is over, and she needs to chill. It's hysterical to watch her process this command. Her head swivels from ottoman to commander; she pauses, not sure she wants to obey. We repeat the command, followed by a finger point toward the ottoman. If she is still not on that ottoman by this time, we issue a stern, extended vocalizing of her name: "Daaaiissssyyyy," which is difficult to do with a straight face. During the escalating command gestures, Daisy will give half committals—a sitting shuffle toward the ottoman, a walk over to the ottoman but then sit on the floor next to it while looking at you, or she will even lift her front paws and chest onto the ottoman with her back legs dangling off, just chillin' out. She will try anything but full committal and look at us as if to say, "This good enough?"

But half committals are not good enough. A woman I worked with years ago used to say, "Half obedience is still disobedience." That hurts, doesn't it? Most often it would never be our intention to disobey our Lord. But are we fully obeying? Are we trying to get away with half committals thinking that is good enough? Are we trying to rework the command hoping to fit it into something more acceptable? Or perhaps we are disregarding God's command entirely, saying yes but never following through, like the second son mentioned above. The good news is that God is patient and forgiving. His arms are always ready to receive our heartfelt repentance. Let us reflect on the areas of our lives where we might be dismissing God's commands, partially or fully. Let us draw near to Him and surrender anything getting in the way of our full obedience.

Let us not be like Daisy, who tries to get away with anything but complete obedience. Let us not be like the first son, who, even though he eventually obeys, does refuse his father initially. Out of great love and gratitude for who God is, and all He has done for us through Jesus, His Son, let us instead be eager to say, "Yes, Father! Right away, Father! Consider it done, Father!" He will fill us with strength to complete His tasks, for His will always has His support.

Loving Father, we thank You for Your great patience and forgiveness toward us. Please continue to grow us in obedience to You and Your Word. Help us fully abide in our Savior, Jesus, with great joy and availability, so that Your work can be done in and through us, for Your glory. In Jesus's Name, *amen.*

Key scriptures:
Mark 12:30
1 Chronicles 29:17–19
John 15
1 Samuel 3

Day 13

Practice Godly Contentment

LIVING IN NEW ENGLAND, WE are no stranger to cold weather. But sometimes the wind is relentless, and it's just too cold to enjoy the big field with Daisy. On such days, Daisy must settle for a twenty-foot leash anchored to our deck in the back of our condo. She can't run the same, but what she loves to do is bring a toy out to play with. It really is funny watching her drop a toy in front of the door and then stare at you as if to say, "Can we go out to play?"

She did just this last Christmas morning. We sent her out with two of her new toys, thinking that she would be entertained for a good while with new toys. We started cooking breakfast as we enjoyed the momentary calm of not chasing Daisy to retrieve wrapping paper from her mouth. Well, the calm did not last long; Daisy's "bullhorn" bark soon interrupted us, just what our neighbors want to hear on Christmas morning! Apparently, the neighbor's three small dogs were outside as well. Daisy was leaning down, butt in the air, squishing her cute face into the six-inch opening between the privacy fence and the grass, trying desperately to get a look next door. She couldn't see her little pals, but she could smell and hear them, hence the barking. Maybe she was saying, "Merry Christmas guys … see my new toys!" But regardless, the barking needed to stop. I ran outside to squeak one of her new toys, which thankfully distracted her. A few moments passed before Daisy's barking returned, this time at a leaf blowing across the snow. I look outside again, exasperated, and questioned, "Can't you just be happy playing with your new toys?!" And I must tell you, not even ten seconds passed before I chuckled at the impression that I had of God turning my own question onto me. He has an amazing way of doing that, doesn't He?

Ah ... contentment. What a beautiful quality to possess. I have it in abundance in some areas of my life, and not nearly enough in other areas. Can you relate? I'm sure we all can to some degree. We see the latest ads for the newest and greatest whatever, catch a glimpse at a fashion-trending movie star, hear about a friend's success, and the seeds of discontentment grow. Why are we so easily distracted, causing who we are and what we have to all of a sudden seem like not enough? I once heard someone say that discontentment was like telling God you are not happy with how He made you or with what He provided. Ouch! It makes me so sad to think that I have said this to my God, but I know in my thoughts and/or actions I have. Praise Him, He is a forgiving God! Through His Word, we learn that true contentment does not come from earthly beauty or possessions but from knowing who God is and who we are in Him. Keep the below scripture verses close and call upon them when discontentment grows. These truths teach us to walk in victory and provide a contentment for our soul, which ultimately fills every other part of our lives.

Heavenly Father, forgive us for our discontentment.
Grow us in gratitude for everything You have given
us, in the spiritual realm as well as the physical.

Make us aware of distractions that cause the seeds of discontentment to work their way into our hearts and minds, and strengthen us to rest in Your perfect provision. In the Name of Jesus we pray, amen.

Key scriptures:
Colossians 2:10
Philippians 4:11–13
Colossians 3:1–4
Psalm 23

Day 14

Welcome God's Peace

WE HAVE LIVED IN NEW England our entire lives, but my husband's desire to move to Florida grows as retirement approaches. I told him Daisy will not be happy if we move down south, as she loves the winter and the colder the better. He rolled his eyes, and I chuckled. But honestly, she just loves the cold. If snow is on the ground, all the better. She runs back and forth, hops up and down like a bunny, and dives her face into an edible pile of flakes. What's hysterical is that when she's playing like this and some snow kicks up as a result, it startles her and she'll pounce on it as if to say, "Hey, where'd you come from?" Then she proceeds to chase it as her pouncing sends the snowball on a roll.

One winter she developed mild frostbite on her back paw. The temperature was colder than normal, so we hadn't stayed out long but apparently too long. I felt terrible. Thankfully, the frostbite was mild, and she healed quickly, but we did need to use the "cone of shame" so she wouldn't lick the area and irritate it more. She did *not* like that, as I'm sure many of you have witnessed with your own pets. She fought me, but once on, she wouldn't move. She stared at me out of the corner of her eyes. Sad little dog. Of course she didn't understand why I was putting the cone on her. She did not know that it was for her own good and that I was doing what was best for her at the moment, because I love her.

Life can be difficult. Forget small daily frustrations, as discussed on day 3. Sometimes life hits so hard that it's difficult to see any good. We question what God is doing. Does He hear our prayers? Does He see what we are going through? Why are things so difficult? We fight our current circumstances because surely life is not supposed to be this way. However, Jesus tells us to expect difficulty. In the Gospel of John, chapter 16, verse 33, Jesus states: "I have told you these things, so that in me you may have peace. In this world you will have trouble. But take heart! I have overcome the world." This is an important verse for us as Christ followers to remember during challenging times. Difficult times are part of our fallen, broken world, but as we focus on Christ, we can still have peace. Because Jesus has overcome, by His grace and through His power, we can too. As we look to Him, as discussed on day 9, our focus comes off our circumstances and rests on His ability to fill us with peace and strength, come what may. The Bible tells us that God works all things for the good of those who love Him (Romans 8:28). He does what is best for us, and, yes, that sometimes means allowing struggles because He sees what can come from the struggle: our correction, perseverance, spiritual maturity, exercised faith amid the difficulty that brings someone else to Jesus. These are the good outcomes only God can bring forth from adversity, because He loves us.

> Father in heaven, we praise You for Your love and
> for sending Jesus who has defeated the broken ways
> of this world. Help us to seek Your peace always
> and to rest in Your ability to redeem and restore.
> Strengthen us to hold your hand through times of

difficulty, knowing You are there, and You always do what is best for us even when we can't see it. In Jesus's Name, *amen*.

Key scriptures:
Ephesians 2:14a
Romans 5:1–5
Psalm 91
Isaiah 26:3
2 Corinthians 4:16–18

Day 15

Relish in God's Unfailing Love

WE LOVE LIVING IN OUR condo, and although I wish Daisy had our previous fenced-in backyard to run around and chase squirrels in, she does not lack exercise even if we don't go outside. You see, our condo is small, but it is nicely sprawled out over four floors of living. And we use our built-in stair master to drain Daisy of that endless energy, especially from six to seven o'clock each night when she tends to have her "feisty fits," as we call them. Like clockwork, Daisy's energy escalates as she jumps on anyone nearby, bites sleeves, and hops on furniture and scratches like a kitten with a scratch post. She will sprint in circles growling deeply. The entire routine took us off guard, as our previous poodle, Buddy, never exhibited this behavior. Apparently, it is so common that it has a name: The zoomies. Yes, that's a real thing! Almost like a toddler who has been overstimulated, Daisy needs to release excess energy before falling asleep. Google stated that zooming occurs because of lack of exercise, but we disagree. Even on days where Daisy is very stimulated and has lots of exercise, she will still zoom. So, we do what we can to help this nightly need pass quickly and safely, for everyone's sake! Usually playing ball will do it, and we will repeatedly throw a toy down the hallway for Daisy to run after and pounce on before she victoriously gathers it up in her mouth and returns it to us. But sometimes this play will not appease the "feisty fit," and our oldest daughter will state, "OK, let's go stair zoom." Daisy follows Rose as she runs up and down our four floors, tossing toys from one level to the other to keep Daisy entertained. They both return exhausted, and we know Daisy's feisty fit is done. She's down for the night, and we all take a relaxing breath as calm settles upon the room.

My family laughs at a saying I have for Daisy: "She's a lot of work!" And she is! She is a high maintenance dog in so many ways. But they can laugh when I say it because they know how much I adore her. I remember during one of Daisy's fits just watching her and wondering what God must be thinking about me when I'm having a feisty fit of my own for whatever reason. And I am certainly high maintenance in many areas as well. I smile as I picture Him saying, "Boy, you're a lot of work today, Josie." Doesn't that make you chuckle? How many times God must shake His head, all the while smiling. And just like we wanted to help Daisy's moment pass quickly and safely for her and for us, God is our helper in times of chaos.

Can you think of your feisty fit moments? Well, God knows what is needed to bring us back to a place of calm. When we are having a fit for whatever reason, let us remember that God does not turn His back. He loves and adores us during these moments, and He stays faithfully by our side until such episodes pass. Amazing, isn't it? Especially since He knows a new episode will most likely occur tomorrow as well. Unfailing love indeed!

Father, Your love and faithfulness endure forever!
Thank You that You are always there for us, in
times of calm as well as times of chaos. Train us

to keep our eyes on You and find peace in Your unfailing love. We ask in Jesus's Name, *amen.*

Key scriptures:
Romans 8:38–39
Psalm 136
Psalm 54:4
Lamentations 3:22–23

It's a new day!

Thank you again for
joining me in

these devotionals. I
pray they bless you

as they have blessed me
and that we all

will grow in our awareness
of the presence

of our loving God in

our everyday moments!

He loves when we recognize

His nearness!

Day 16

Persevere with Godly Trust

REMEMBER THOSE STAIRS WE TALKED about yesterday? Our built-in stair master that we use to drain Daisy's energy? Well, she hasn't always embraced those stairs with reckless abandon. When Daisy was just a puppy, she was quite intimidated by our endless mountain of stairs. We, of course, carried her when she was smaller than the stair height itself, but as she grew, she learned to climb up confidently. Coming down, however, was another matter. One day Daisy was playing nicely on the top level while I was putting things away. With my mind occupied, I started to walk down the stairs, forgetting about Daisy's current fear of the downward staircase. She startled me with her bark, "No way, Mom!" I decided it was time for her to conquer this fear. I mean, she was older, larger, and definitely did not lack the strength or the determination that going down the stairs would take. It was new to her, so she just lacked the confidence. As her mamma, I knew if she would just try it once, she would realize she could do it, and then there would be no stopping her. So it was my job to encourage her into it. I stayed halfway down the first flight of stairs, bent over and used my sweetest voice, "Come on, girl, you can do it; come to Mamma." She immediately backed up, barked louder, and assumed a downward dog position. Tail still raised, however, so I kept encouraging her with a smile on my face and enthusiasm in my voice. Daisy would approach the first step, wanting to believe me. But she was hesitant. For a good five minutes she would approach, then back up, approach, then back up, over and over. And yes, the barking persisted the entire time. I should have inserted ear plugs before I began this training! Eventually she came down one step. Looking up at me, she did another step, and then another. Suddenly she jumped the last three steps. I don't know if she mustered the energy out of excitement for her victory, or if she was trying to complete this task as quickly as possible, but either way she continued down the next set of steps with no problem, so proud of herself. I just stayed where I was and watched her do her thing, smiling at her achievement. I knew she could do it, and I knew she would prove to herself she could do it if she just tried.

Is there something you would like to do, maybe even something you need to do or something you feel God directing you to do, but you are afraid to take the first step? Fear is quite the disabling force. The Bible records God telling us numerous times to not fear. I like that God acknowledges that fear is real. He is not saying we will never face fear. Instead, His command to not fear is a reminder that we do not *need* to fear. If we do a study on this topic, we will see that contextually the reason we do not need to fear is because God is with us. He is bigger than our fear, greater than our hesitancy, stronger than the struggle. Our courage does not come from our ability but from His. His plan for us can be unknown and scary to step out into, but He wants our faith to overtake our fear. Just like I was there for Daisy, encouraging her and standing by to support and protect, God is there for us when we are afraid, when we feel ill-equipped and insecure. As our encourager, He is always cheering us on when we trust instead of tremble.

> Father in Heaven, forgive us when we are frozen
> by fear, when our eyes are on the difficulty or
> the unknown instead of on You who can do
> all things. Grow us in Your command to not
> fear and in our faith that You are greater. Help
> us walk in the confidence of Your presence.
> We praise You! In Jesus's Name, *amen.*

Key scriptures:
Isaiah 41:10
Joshua 1:9
Psalm 46

Day 17

Focus on God's Blessings

PRACTICING GRATITUDE IS SO BENEFICIAL, mentally as well as physically. The thoughts we entertain in our mind have a direct impact on the level of inflammation in our physical body. It's true. Dr. Bruce Lipton shares in his book *The Biology of Belief* how negative thoughts have been shown to increase bodily inflammation, while positive, grateful thoughts decrease inflammation. Isn't that amazing?! Shortly after becoming a believer, I learned the importance of mental journaling. This involves talking to God and listing all for which you are grateful. A form of prayer, for sure, but with a focus on gratitude and the recalling of blessings received. Often while writing I will take a break to pray and collect my thoughts. I begin mental journaling, thanking God for the day, for His direction and guidance with each day's devotional, for the quiet of my home so I can focus, for the sunshine streaming through the kitchen window, and on and on. I've never been one to write my thoughts in a paper journal. I know many who do, and they love it, but I never stuck with it. Mental journaling, however, has become a daily practice. In good times and in struggles, it keeps God's many blessings sharp in my mind and emboldens me to continue to trust Him with all things.

You will recall me telling you on day 15 about how much work Daisy is. If these high-maintenance moments line up with my stressful, busy, or tired moments, seeds of annoyance can settle in. Suddenly my mind races with grumbles and complaints about her busyness, her care needs, how I didn't want another dog, this was the girls' idea, etc., etc. Yup, it's true—my mind is not a pretty place sometimes. I know everyone can relate. Inevitably I feel terrible about my thoughts because I know that's not how I really feel; I truly adore her. It's the stress or exhaustion talking, and as soon as I calm her down or meet whatever need is pressing, I practice deep breathing to calm my mind and turn to my mental journaling, beginning with repentance over my lack of gratitude for this amazing dog God has granted us. Then, I start saying truths: listing all the things I love about her and thanking God for all the ways she has been a blessing in our lives.

The enemy loves to whisper disgruntled thoughts to us, doesn't he? He loves to distract us away from God's goodness and for us to focus on negativity instead. It's perfectly normal for us to get annoyed or have a negative thought; we are human remember. But it's what we entertain, linger on, and let settle in our heart and mind that can grow either displeasure or gratitude. We must be on guard against Satan's lies and our own weakness during times of stress, busyness, and fatigue. We must pray for awareness during these weak moments and for strength to change our mental focus. If you haven't practiced mental journaling, I encourage you to try it. It has been a game changer for me, bringing peace, truth, and joy into my daily moments. It fights lies, negativity, stress, self-focus, and inflammation! It also honors

God so much, who instructs us in His Word to, "forget not all His benefits" (Psalm 103:1–5).

Truth-full, Father, You alone see into the hearts
and minds of man, and we are sorry when we get
distracted away from truth. Grow our awareness of
the enemy's lies and deceptions and make us strong to
focus on You. Help us to remember the connection
between our thoughts and our physical well-being
and develop an attitude of gratitude within us that
will bless us mentally as well as physically. Strip us of
grumbling and complaining as we recall all that You
have done for us. We praise You for Your incredible
grace. We ask in Your Son's holy Name, *amen.*

Key scriptures:
Philippians 2:14, 4:8
Proverbs 17:22
Nehemiah 8:10
Psalm 66:16

Day 18

Cooperate with God's Work

SO MANY JOYS COME WITH welcoming a new puppy into your home. Potty training, however, is not one of them. It is exhausting! At least with a baby you can put a diaper on him or her, right?! Once Daisy was potty trained, we decided to let her sleep outside of her crate at night. We rushed to the pet store and purchased a large, comfy bed for her. She likes to sleep not curled up but sprawled out in a straight line, so she needs lots of room. We placed her new throne aside our bed and rubbed it with one of my sweatshirts, so it would smell like Mamma and bring her comfort. She must be pleased with the arrangement because she has always stayed on her bed at night. She's a great sleeper, thank God—must be from all that pre-bed zooming!

One night I woke to nails clicking on the hardwoods. Next, I felt hot breath on my face and opened my eyes to see Daisy aside of me, hanging out with her front legs up on my bed. The last thing I wanted to do was get out from under my warm covers just to bring her back to her bed. I was so tempted to give in and say, "Up," but I knew long term that would not be good. Poodles are so smart that if they get away with something once, it becomes their new norm. So I dragged my groggy self out of bed and led Daisy back to her resting place, commanding her to stay.

As I began to doze off, I once again heard nail clanging on the floor. "What is she doing?" I asked myself. I'm quite surprised as this has never been an issue for her before. I knew she didn't have to go to the bathroom, as she stands by the bedroom door when she needs to go out. Instead she was coming over to me, standing on back legs with front legs on my bed once again. There was no doubt she wanted to snuggle. Apparently her six-inch thick, twice her size, orthopedic bed is no longer good enough!

She was testing me. She knew where she was supposed to rest but challenged the limits anyway. Oh, and it almost worked. I had a battle going on in my mind, which was only half awake remember. "Do I let her up? Just this once. What's the harm? No, no I can't. She'll never go back to her own bed. And hubby will not be happy. Get up, woman. Be patient and gentle. Ugh!" So once again I exited the warmth of my bed and escorted Daisy back to her spot. I rubbed her softly and told her to stay. This time it sticks. Thank you, Lord!

The next day I was telling my daughter about Daisy's nighttime adventure, and it occurred to me: How many times do I test the Lord when I know what to do but don't do it? Can you relate? I'm sure there are areas in our lives where we challenge God's limits, and He must keep reinforcing the right thing. I know things would go a lot smoother for us if we cooperated faster, right?! But we are human, and we like to impart our will over His sometimes, even unintentionally. When our girls were young, I stayed home with them and would catch myself overriding something Daddy had determined. Not with any desire to supersede my husband, but simply because of being home to deal with the daily decisions. I felt conviction in this area as God reminded me how to honor my husband by supporting his word. Yes, we all need God's gentle reminders in what is right and good. We are all a work in progress, that's for sure. I praise Him for His Word, which teaches us what is right, and for His Holy Spirit who guides us in His ways. As discussed on day 10, God is patient with us, and He knows how many times it is going to take before we really learn a lesson. Sadly, it is often more than the two times it took Daisy to learn to stay on her bed. But two or twenty-two, God is love, and therefore God is patient.

> Almighty God, thank You so much for Your great
> love and patience with us. You are the change we
> need, and we praise You for never giving up on us.
> Forgive us when we do not obey what we know
> to do and for testing the limits. Please grow us in
> both big and small issues and fill us with a desire to
> cooperate with the work You are doing in our lives.
> In Jesus's holy Name, *amen.*

Key scriptures:
Psalm 32:8
John 14:26
2 Timothy 3:16
1 Corinthians 13:4–8a

Day 19

Walk in God's Newness

OUR OLDEST DAUGHTER IS A schoolteacher, and the school she works at welcomes teachers to bring their dogs to work with them. You've heard of "Bring your child to work day?" Well, Rose's school has an ongoing "Teacher bring your dog to school day." And it's wonderful. Not only does it prevent the dog from being home alone all day, but it teaches their students to care for a pet while also providing a calming influence on children needing a moment of comfort. Lucky Daisy! Rose prepared her for this school adventure, gathering a water bottle, treats, toys, and most importantly, the gentle leader. Have you ever used a gentle leader? It is a miracle worker! For anyone unfamiliar with this tool, it is a leash that has an additional section that circles around the nose. Apparently, dogs have a spot on the bridge of their nose that, when pressed, calms them. So our very energetic, often rambunctious, poodle becomes compliant and calm with the simple placement of some black rope around her nose. Genius! We don't use it often as it's only needed if Daisy will be around a lot of other people or dogs. She just listens better, and her calm demeanor makes whatever event we are attending with her more enjoyable. So we knew Daisy's school day adventure would require the gentle leader.

Now, I knew if Rose used the gentle leader that she would have a wonderful time with Daisy. And there was no doubt Daisy would have the time of her life. Lots of people, other dogs, small kids all around—Heaven for Daisy! I smiled just thinking of how much fun she was about to have. But not all our family members were thrilled. They expressed concern over Daisy's energy and jumping habits—"silly Daisy behavior" we like to say. True concerns for sure. But they hadn't participated in Daisy's daily training to the same degree as I had or witnessed the strides she had taken in her obedience. They also hadn't taken Daisy to crowded places. I've seen her behave like a show dog among busy crowds, so I knew she would be fine. They had in mind the old, untrained, wild Daisy and therefore advised against bringing her, saying she wasn't ready, she would be wild, she could hurt someone, etc.

Rose knew exactly how to handle Daisy with the gentle leader and how to command her softly and confidently. I knew if Rose set the expectations right away, Daisy would rise to them. And she did! Daisy was so obedient and didn't jump on anyone— huge achievement for our bouncing puppy. She stayed right with Rose, and they had a wonderful day together.

Second Corinthians 5:17 states: "Therefore, if anyone is in Christ, he is a new creation; the old has gone, the new has come!" Praise Jesus for this truth! I rest in who I now am in Him and know without any doubt that who I was before Him is gone forever. This is a gift given to us by the Father when we accept His Son as Savior. All our sins, weaknesses, failures, etc. are gone. Now, we might still deal with some of these sins, weaknesses, and failures, but they no longer have victory over us. We are not defined by them, nor do we suffer eternally because of them. Jesus's victory on the cross on our behalf is what defines us. We are new in Him! We know this to be true, but sometimes people who knew the "old" us don't always allow us to walk in this new life. Like a bad image that won't leave our minds, they bring up the past as if it still applied. They attribute what was as if it was still, failing to recognize the change Jesus has caused.

We must cling to scripture, always, but especially when our past keeps surfacing. Memorize the above passage, saying it as often as needed to combat people's desires, intentionally or not, to keep us in past failures. Or sometimes we are that person, right? We can just as often be the one not allowing another, or ourselves, to walk in the new freedom found in Christ. We must remember, if the Son sets us free, we are all free *indeed*! (John 8:36).

Gracious God, what a gift we have in Jesus who
wipes away our darkness and fills us with His light.
Thank You for making us new. Strengthen us to
walk in this newness, letting go of the past. Help our
lives reflect Your transforming power and thereby
allow those around us to see the change You make
so they may be made new as well. Through Your
Spirit and for Your glory, in Jesus's Name, *amen*.

Key scriptures:
Isaiah 43:18–19
Ezekiel 36:26–27
Galatians 2:20

Day 20

Stand Secure on God's Foundation

I LOVE SUMMERTIME! YES, THE sun and warmth are welcomed, but the main reason I love this season so much is because our daughters are home. Our eldest, a teacher, has the summers off from full-time work, and our youngest, a college student, is home rather than on campus. We have always been a close family, so their presence brings so much joy to our home. And boy does Daisy love the busyness! She must go into culture shock as she transitions from quiet mom-only days to a house consistently full of family and friends. More people to play with, more people to walk her … yay for her, and truthfully, yay for me!

One summer night our youngest daughter Faith and I were in our family room watching a movie. As always, Daisy was resting aside of me. Faith and I both recognized Daisy's resting position; flat on her back, head bent sideways 90 degrees, back legs spread wide open, with front legs in the air and bent, giving her best T-Rex imitation. We chuckled hard. Then we marveled at our sweet puppy. You see, Daisy's dog trainer explained that this exact position signals complete submission by a dog. It is the most vulnerable posture a dog can be in. She obviously feels no threat or hesitation to be vulnerable with us as she lay there all exposed. The elementary school our girls attended strived for every student to feel "save, wanted and loved." I recalled this as I watched Daisy rest. She most definitely felt safe, wanted, and loved, and it made Faith and I smile.

Daisy often strikes this T-Rex pose, and it reminds me to thank God that we are all safe, wanted, and loved by Him. Through Jesus our Savior, we can rest with the Father exposed but with no fear. We can appear before Him naked, but with no shame, needy but not hopeless, unworthy but covered by His love. Today's devotional is an encouragement for us to reflect on these truths and smile. Let our hearts be filled with joy that Jesus has brought us such love and freedom, and may these joys be our strength today.

Loving God, thank You for welcoming us before
Your throne of grace because of all Your Son did
for us. In Him we are Your children and praise
You for making us feel so safe, so wanted, so
loved. May we walk in these truths today with
joy and gratitude. In Jesus's Name, *amen.*

Key scriptures:
2 Thessalonians 3:3
Ephesians 1:1–14
John 3:16

Day 21

Turn to God, Our Shield and Warrior

I LOVE TO WATCH THE *Dog Whisperer.* Have you seen that
show? Cesar Millan is a well-known and respected dog trainer,
especially for troubled big breeds such as pit bulls or German
shepherds. He advises owners to provide rules, boundaries, and
limitations for their dogs so that they learn well and feel secure.
He also advises owners to not coddle their dog when they are
experiencing anxiety or fear. Instead, he recommends the owner
give confident guidance through the anxious or fearful moment.
I remembered this training when Daisy and I were on a walk one
day, and she freaked out when a trash bucket was blown over by
the wind. The noise sent my sweet puppy into a fearful fit as she
pulled against her leash and jumped up on her back paws like a
startled stallion. Her front paws were reaching out to me, as if
doggie paddling through the air. It was quite a sight but not in
a humorous way. I knew she was afraid. I tried to confidently
correct the situation, guiding her back to all fours and past the
bucket with encouraging words and leash control, but Daisy
wouldn't have it. She was frozen: up on her back legs again with a
death grip around my torso with her front legs. More encouraging
words and a retreat in the direction we came from allowed Daisy
to relax and resume her joyful walk. Mind you, her head swiveled
repeatedly behind her to ensure that mean ol' trash bucket wasn't

following. To this day, she is afraid of those big black cylinders. When we walk on trash day, we make exaggerated efforts to avoid all trash cans. She doesn't always strike the startled stallion pose, but I remain ready to verbally coach her past any bucket in sight as she pulls in the opposite direction or when she runs quickly up close to my leg for refuge. She remembers how I helped her through that first experience. I was her shield, her protector. She's confident I would be again if that nasty trash bucket came rolling her way once more.

Oh, how many times I have been worked up with anxiety or frozen by fear. Even though I bring them to the Lord, the same anxieties and fears often appear over and over. Can you relate? Once Satan knows we struggle in an area, he loves to keep bringing it to our attention. However, scripture refers to God as our help and our shield (Psalm 28:7). But whereas it took me a bit to figure out what Daisy needed and the best way to handle the situation, God always knows the perfect remedy, every time. We just need to turn to Him, and quickly. We can doggie paddle our way to Him, and He will always be there to shield and protect. In prayer and through His Word, we receive truths that are our weapon against the attacks of fear and anxiety. They are our "leash" that gently guides us to truth. I love that the Bible also refers to God as our Warrior (Exodus 15:3). Can't you picture Him? With unlimited power and authority, He fights for us. He shoots His arrows and scatters our enemies (Psalm 18:14). This Warrior is also our gentle guide who leads our hearts and minds back to the path of victory as we focus on Him. Let us memorize the below scriptures and call upon them at such times so we relax in the face of anxiety and fear and resume our joyful walk with our Lord.

All powerful Father, we praise You that You fight on
our behalf. You lead us beside still waters, and You
guide us in the way everlasting. As we go through
our day, please fill our minds with Your truths and
strengthen us to use them to guide our day. Help us
to recognize when anxiety and fear are rising and be
quick to turn to You, knowing You are always there,
always able. We ask in Jesus's holy Name, *amen.*

Key scriptures:
1 Peter 5:7
Isaiah 26:3
Ephesians 6:10–18
Zephaniah 3:17

Day 22

Seek God's Direction

AS YOU KNOW, DAISY AND I walk each day. She loves meeting other dogs and is always so excited when she spots another four-legged friend. I'll ask the owner if we can say hello, and Daisy is just chomping at the bit to get the okay. Her tail starts wagging excitedly, she runs up to her new friend, and they circle each other and exchange hellos. If the situation is right, they'll get to run and play. They are dogs; this is what they do.

When we are faced with new experiences, daily decisions, and life distractions, how do we know what we are to do? With dogs, their behavior is mostly innate. Training and life experiences do contribute, but for the most part they don't need to think about the above interaction; it's just what they do. But with us humans, innately, we rely on ourselves, speak without thought, act with selfish ambitions, and shy away from what might be new or different (well, maybe this last one applies to just some of us). These are our innate, self-focused responses that cause us to greatly fall short and even get us into trouble! However, scripture once again guides us in what to do. It tells us to not lean on our own understanding and to not be wise in our own eyes (Proverbs 3:5–7). Rather we are to seek the Lord always, to lean on Him and on His ways (1 Chronicles 16:11). Doing so promises wisdom and guidance in our new experiences and with the daily issues we face. Doing so also helps us learn what pleases our heavenly Father. The more time we spend with God in prayer and in His Word, the more we are shaped away from our innate, sinful nature and back into His image. Our desires start to line up with His, and our innate self-focus becomes altered by the fruit of the Holy Spirit. This is a powerful work of God, and when we seek His face, He changes us and reveals the way we should go.

All Wise One, we thank You for Your open-ended invitation to come and learn from You and for Your incredible power to change the likes of us. Thank You that You give wisdom generously and for always being there to lovingly guide us. Give us ears to hear Your direction, for You know every detail, and we welcome Your intervention. In Jesus's Name, amen.

Key scriptures:
Jeremiah 29:11–13
2 Chronicles 20:12
Psalm 119:9, 105
James 1:5
Galatians 5:22–25, 6:8–9
Titus 3:3–8

Day 23

Rest in God's Shadow

MY HUSBAND LOVES TO PARTICIPATE in the Sports Ministry at our church. During the summertime, we find ourselves at the ball field on Sunday nights enjoying the beautiful weather and cheering him on as he plays softball. The field our church plays on is one of three fields behind a local elementary school, which also offers a track, a play gym, and swings. The area is often bustling with children playing, people walking their dogs, and other teams of various sorts practicing. This is an exciting time for Daisy! The first time we brought her, she didn't know where to look first. Needless to say, she tugged and pulled, whined and barked, and darted from one stimulus to another. I put her on a shorter leash and guided her alongside me as I walked around the track while keeping an eye on my husband's game. I figured this would drain Daisy's energy and tire her out some—and give my arm a break from the tugging! My efforts were successful until I decided to stand near my husband's field position and watch the game. Every time my husband would run to catch the ball, Daisy would bark incessantly and attempt to run with him. You can just hear her bark stating, "Wait for me, Dad, I want to play too." She definitely didn't appreciate the fence blocking her from doing so! I just laughed but realized this might not be so cute to the others watching the game, so I took Daisy to our truck to watch the event from there. Silence settled on the field. Ahhhhh.

This silence did not fill our truck, however. Despite my attempts to quiet her, Daisy would not stop whining. And she wouldn't settle into the passenger seat. She kept trying to climb over the center console and step onto my lap. I'm thinking she wants to look out my window because it is closer to Daddy's position on the field. I tell her no because the steering wheel is in the way, and her paws would dig into my thighs—not too comfortable for Mamma! This continued off and on for an hour! Finally I gave in. (Bad mom, I know, but the whining was really bothering my daughter and I). I'm certain her vocals will stop if she can just look out the window. What does she do? She doesn't step over me to see out my window but instead climbs her forty-one pound body on me and sits in my lap. Whining stops as she leans her body into my chest, squeezed in between me and the steering wheel. She sits in silence and watches the game. I remember taking a deep breath and just hugging her. My love for my sweet baby girl Daisy grew even more in that moment. You see, she didn't just want to get her way and move into my seat because it was her will. She wanted the security and assurance that came from being close to me (real close, apparently). Perhaps all the stimuli was a bit much for her. I do believe she enjoyed it, as she loves people, but I believe all the excitement made her anxious, which made her feel overwhelmed. She is a bit anxious in nature to begin with. My family and I have seen this in her on several occasions, and each time she looks to be close to those who provide safety. I was happy to oblige.

Do you know that your loving heavenly Father is happy to oblige you when assurance and safety are needed? Indeed He is! Psalm 91:1 states: "He who dwell in the shelter of the Most High will rest in the shadow of the Almighty." You must be nice and close to someone to have their shadow cast on you. If the sun had been able to penetrate the roof of our truck, Daisy most certainly would have been in my shadow. Up close and personal undoubtedly describes Daisy. And God invites us to be up close and personal with Him, always. I love how the Psalm says we will "rest" in God's shadow, not stand or sit or find His shadow, but rest! To rest implies comfort, peace, and calm. To rest means our anxieties and stressors do not hold us captive. Instead, we have the assurance that our God can protect and calm.

We get up close and personal with God through His Son, Jesus Christ, our Savior, who made a way for us to draw near to the Father. To "dwell in the shelter of the Lord" means to live with and for God, to enter His presence each day, each moment even, and to obey His house rules. We must read His Word, practice prayer and worship, and train our eyes to see Him in everyday moments. Let us draw near today, knowing there is no substitute for the rest found in His shadow.

> Almighty God, thank You so much for Your
> open arms of assurance and safety. You calm
> us like no other Father. May You continue to
> train us to draw near each day, and may we
> always find great comfort and peace in resting
> in Your shadow. In Jesus's Name, *amen.*

Key scriptures:
Psalm 91
Psalm 36:7
Matthew 11:28–30

Day 24

Search God with a Curious Heart

IN OUR TOWNHOUSE, WE HAVE three large picture windows all in a row, making a wall of beautiful sunrise light that brightens our living room. A sense of warmth comes upon me every time I enter this space. Daisy must feel it too, as the living room is her favorite daytime spot. Well, maybe it's not the light or the warmth that draws Daisy in but rather the view from these large windows. She can see everything: Traffic driving by, people walking, and, most importantly, other dogs being walked or playing on the grassy common area. Whenever someone in the house asks where Daisy is, I respond, "She's on neighborhood watch," and sure enough we can look in the living room and find her perched up on "her" ottoman staring out these windows. So curious about everything, her head will dart from left to right constantly. It's hysterical. I love that even when in a different room, I can tell what Daisy sees by her vocalizations. If Daisy whines, I know she sees another dog she wishes she could go out and play with. If I hear a single bark repeated but spread out, I learn that someone Daisy recognizes is walking in the area. If I hear a growl, the UPS or Amazon driver has approached. And excited barking followed by a jump off the ottoman means a member of her household is home, and she is running to the door to greet them (with a body slam hello no doubt). She is captivated by every sight and sound.

One spring day while exhibiting her usual nosy neighbor tendencies, Daisy was entertained by the birds in our front bushes. She scurried from one window to the next trying to follow them as they hopped along the ground looking for food or perhaps nest scraps. Who would not be distracted by this adorable sight? I was, and I remember saying a quick prayer that I would be as curious about God and His Word as Daisy is about her surroundings.

It thrills our heavenly Father when we are curious about Him! A prayer I pray routinely is for Him to take me deeper: deeper in my knowledge of Him, deeper in my understanding of His Word and ways, deeper in my love and gratitude, and deeper in my reflection of my Savior, Jesus. I pray this because we can get stuck in our routines even when it comes to reading and praying, can't we? Our lives are busy with so many daily obligations that our time with God can get routine as well. If you deal with this too, join me in the above prayer, knowing God will most definitely grow us in these areas. Then, let us take steps to deepen our knowledge of Him. Let's not just read the Word but meditate on what we've read and listen for His Holy Spirit to whisper revelations into our hearts and minds. When I became a believer, I purchased a commentary to aid in my learning. Now I will still turn to it, looking for knowledge and context regarding what I am reading. Although no one can enlighten us like the Holy Spirit can (John 14:26), a commentary shares wisdom and revelations others have received. It is a great resource, and I always come away with a deeper understanding of the scripture I just read.

Jeremiah 33:3 states: "'Call to me and I will answer you and tell you great and unsearchable things you do not know.'" Christ is the greatest unsearchable thing. I praise God for showing Him to me. And I know that, through Christ, He has more treasures for me to discover. Will you join me in praying for curious hearts and deeper knowledge? Let us be on "neighborhood watch" and thrilled by every sight and sound His truth reveals!

> Unsearchable Creator, God, You are so gracious
> to us in welcoming us to know You. Grow our
> curiosity for You and take us deeper, Father.
> Forgive us when we read Your Word or enter
> Your presence distracted, half-hearted or rushed.
> Teach us to sit and be still and to hear Your Holy
> Spirit who reminds us of all You have said. Help
> us make You our priority and grant us wisdom and
> revelation so we may know You better and reflect
> You more. We ask in Jesus's holy Name, *amen.*

Key scriptures:
Colossians 2:2–3
Proverbs 2:1–5
2 Peter 3:18

Day 25

Reflect God's Beauty

MOST WOMEN THAT I KNOW love going to the salon to have their hair cut. It provides a break from our day-to-day obligations and an hour or two of total relaxation. Poodles need monthly "spa days" as their coats grow as quickly as human hair. However, I can't say Daisy looks as favorably upon these days as I do. She is very unhappy with Mamma and tries to cling to me as we approach the front door of her groomer. But I know how necessary it is to keep that poodle hair and skin neat, so I gently urge her on as I hand the leash over to her equally encouraging stylist. I know she will do fine, and I can't wait to pick her up. There's something so wonderful about that clean, trimmed coat on the groomed day. She feels like a thick, fleece blanket, and she looks like such a "poodle" sporting her pom-pom tail, shaved paws and bows in her ears. Our last poodle, Buddy, was a boy, so we just kept his grooming simple. Now that we have a girl, I love that her groomer "poodles her up" as I like to say. But that very night Daisy is back to wrestling with my husband as if the WWF championship is at stake. Yup, dolled up or not, she's the same silly Daisy!

First Samuel 16:7b instructs us that the heart of a person is of concern to God, not one's outward appearance. God loves us no matter what we look like. Just like Daisy came home and played and wrestled consistent with her true nature, completely unaware of her new do and stylish bows, so can we be before God and others. As Jesus's followers, we know that our identity rests in Him. Memorizing scripture about who He says we are frees us from focusing too much on our appearance and on what others think of us. Now sure, it is perfectly fine to want to look and be at our best. We want our inner light from Jesus to shine through our external appearance, actions, words, works, etc. But we don't want our external appearance to grab our heart. Regardless of our outward glitz or glamour, it is the heart that matters to God. I pray that we all, men and women alike, can be as proud and comfortable with ourselves whether we are decked out in our Sunday best or unshowered and wearing our jammie day sweats. This confidence comes from Christ alone—what He thinks of us, and the knowledge that we are complete in Him. How do we grow this confidence? Only through spending time with Him: Through prayer and His Word. By dismissing the standards of this world and filling our minds with His truths. As we do this, one moment at a time, our minds will be made new. We will rest in what our Creator says and thinks, and our confidence will grow.

> Loving Father, we know You see right into our
> hearts so we pray, Lord, that You would continue
> to create within us a pure heart, a heart focused
> on You and the truth of Your Word. Help us not
> be distracted by the external and to not place our
> value in what we look like or how we present
> ourselves. Grow our knowledge of our identity

in Christ our Savior, and may that always be
our first focus. We ask in His Name, *amen.*

Key scriptures:
Colossians 2:10
2 Corinthians 5:17
Romans 12:2
1 Peter 3:3–4

Day 26

Rejoice in God's Opinion

LIVING IN NEW ENGLAND, WE see four clear seasons, and although autumn is my favorite, there's something so beautiful about the newness of spring. After months of barren trees and freezing temperatures, the soul is so ready for the warmth of the sun and the beautiful colors that start appearing on bushes and trees. Sometimes, however, the weather is deceptive. You can look out your window and see the bright sun and think you're stepping out into total warmth when in reality a cold northern breeze sends a chill through your body. As we locals say, "That's New England for you."

Now Daisy, who does not like the hot weather, embraces that chilly breeze wholeheartedly. One day we were out for a walk on just such a day. I felt the warmth of the sun on my arms one moment only to turn my back to the freezing wind the next moment. Shivering, I looked at Daisy who embraced that breeze willingly. She did not turn her back but looked straight into the wind's direction, head lifted high, eyes closed, and poodle ears bouncing in the breeze. She just makes me laugh! Undoubtedly invigorated by the cold air, she started zooming full force in circles around me, while still on a leash mind you. I know that others who witnessed this must think she is absolutely wild, and she is at times, as you've read about.

But this truth about her character just makes me adore her all the more.

This memory with her made me think about how I see my sweet baby girl Daisy versus how strangers must see her in such moments. Others witnessing her leash zooms see just one moment in time. They think she's plain wild and tend to steer away if they don't know her well. Whereas I see her completely. I see her leash zoom as a fun time for her where she embraced the breeze and released energy, *lots* of energy! I see her curiosity at every little thing: Birds, a blowing leaf, a roaring motorcycle going by. I also see her vulnerability when that motorcycle gets too close, and the noise scares her. I see her stubborn defiance but also her tender, cuddle moments when she wants all forty-one pounds sprawled across my lap. I see her personality in totality and as a result love her even more.

This is how God sees us. He sees us completely. In our chaotic, wild moments? Yes! And our heavenly Father loves us in these moments just the same as He does in our calm moments. He sees us in our quiet, reflective Bible times as well as in our stressed, fearful, anxious times. He sees us in our bold moments standing up for Him but also in our insecure moments when we shrink back. He sees us in our fits of anger as well as when we're peacemakers. He is El Roi, the God who sees us. And He loves us through and through. Psalm 139 teaches us that our Creator, God, intimately knows every part of us: the many distinct aspects of our personalities comprised of strengths as well as weaknesses. Others might only see one aspect of our makeup, but this one aspect does not give a full picture of who we are. They may make a judgment about us based solely on this one aspect. Or perhaps we do the judging based on a limited knowledge of someone else? God sees us in totality. He knows us intimately and loves us completely. May we rest in His intimacy and grow in confidence because of being fearfully and wonderfully made (Psalm 139:14). Likewise, may we have a new appreciation of others and the uniqueness with which they too have been created.

Creator, God, thank You for knowing us so
completely and for loving us in the chaotic as well as
in the calm. Grow our appreciation of our uniqueness
and help us rest in what You say about us. Help us
to use our talents for Your glory, and grow us in our
areas of weakness. Forgive us when we pass judgment
on others, and guide us in extending the grace we
desire to receive ourselves. In Jesus's Name, *amen.*

Key scriptures:
Psalm 139
Genesis 16:13–14
John 15:12

Day 27

Grow in God's Spirit

YESTERDAY WE TALKED ABOUT GOD'S intimate knowledge of every aspect of our being. Personally, I'm so glad He knows me so well. Better than anyone, truly. God sees our innermost thoughts, desires, fears, and insecurities. He knows our intricate makeup: Are we an extrovert or more introverted? Do we have the gift of hospitality, or do we prefer to serve behind the scenes? Are we artistic or more analytical? A peacemaker or do we deal with anger? He made us all so differently, and it is a testament to His endless creativity. We don't have to pretend to be anyone other than who He made us to be. He accepts us as is and loves us fully.

Now, of course, we all have areas in need of growth. We are human after all, born with a sin nature, and this sinful nature can interfere with the good work God would like to do in and through us. For example, I am naturally an introvert, happy to stay at home any and even every day. If I'm not careful, I can get very selfish with my time, forgetting it is God who gives me every minute of life. My days are not really my own; they belong to Him, and He has a purpose for me that can't fully be achieved if I'm tucked away by myself each day. This selfish desire to covet my time needs to bow to God's plan for my day and His refining work through His Spirit. Jesus does meet us and saves us right where we are, but once we accept Him as our Savior, we must cooperate with this refinement work. Becoming more like Jesus is a lifelong journey of allowing God to work within us, changing us so we reflect His Son. Just like I need to be faithful to train Daisy and teach her what is acceptable in our home, toward strangers, etc., God is faithful through His Spirit, His Word, and His people, to teach us what pleases Him and how to live so we accurately reflect Jesus. This is a process of dying to self so God's Spirit can reign in our lives. We don't need to try, try, try or do, do, do. When we focus on "trying harder" or "doing more," we are still relying on self. Instead, we need to "seek more," trusting God and His faithfulness to complete His good work in us (Philippians 1:6). As we seek, God grows our knowledge of Him, and our spiritual walk matures. May we consider it an immense joy to learn from Him, diving deep into His Word each day and praying for Him to fine tune our ears to His Spirit's voice so we may hear and perceive what He is doing. May we pray each day for Him to fill us up with Himself, so we not only have all we need to reflect our Savior, but so God will overflow and spill out onto those around us so they too may know Him.

Intimate Father, praise You for the truth of Your
Word, which continually tells us of Your great
love. Thank You that You work within our hearts
and lives enabling us to reflect Jesus to the world,
so that others may know Your love as well. May
we be faithful to seek You, learn from You, and
cooperate with Your will. Strengthen us to die

to self and to walk in Your Spirit and bring You glory. We pray in Jesus's holy Name, *amen*.

Key scriptures:
1 Thessalonians 5:23–24
2 Corinthians 3:18
Galatians 2:20
Ephesians 5:8–10

Day 28

Enjoy God's Daily Moments

DAISY IS NOW TWO YEARS old. Boy, time flies, doesn't it? We look at her now and chuckle, remembering her five-pound frame when we first brought her home. She has been such a joy to our family, a blessing from God indeed! I reflect on the daily devotionals shared in this book and think, "Yup, this is life with Daisy." Sometimes we experience a peaceful, cuddle moment and other times we are pulling our hair out as we withstand a "feisty fit" expressed by our exhausted pup. Daisy has drawn us closer to the Lord as He reminds us of His presence, His character, and His ways through our daily life with her. These reminders cause us to be "in the moment."

I think about my Daisy stories and thank God for allowing me to "see." So many times I go through the day physically busy and mentally distracted. I know I often miss what God might want to show me—the whispers of His Holy Spirit that I don't hear or that I dismiss as my own thoughts. So I praise God for allowing me to receive the lessons He has shown me through my sweet baby girl Daisy. These lessons brought a deeper awareness of His presence in simple, daily life moments. I just love that! I absolutely am in awe of our God as I stand on a beach and marvel at the powerful ocean in front of me. Or as I hike with my family and look out across the amazing view the summit provides. But these past two years with Daisy have increased my understanding that God is in the everyday: the moments easily dismissed as we go about our to-do list, the joys and the pains, the struggles and the ease. He sees our every day and deeply cares about our experiences here. He is all around us and always about His work (John 5:17).

I once read that a great way to start one's day is to pray not for what God can do for us but rather what we can do for Him. As we go about today, let us pray for eyes to see Him and for a heart that is open to what He would like to say to us and to do through us. Let us put away distractions and be present in our daily, mundane moments knowing that God can grant great revelations through them. May we smile at His faithfulness, find joy in His truths revealed, be strengthened through the struggles, derive peace from His unending love, feel conviction from His corrections, and express gratitude for His forgiveness through His Son, Jesus our Savior. He is near!

> Heavenly Father, who are we that You would desire to show Yourself to us as we go about the simplicities and complexities of life. We praise You that You are not a God that is far off, but rather an intimate, personal God who walks through each day with us as we tackle our to-do's. We thank You for Your moments of grace, where You reveal Yourself deeper to us. Grant us eyes to see You and ears to hear You, Father, that we may know You better and rest in Your nearness. In Jesus's Name, *amen.*

Key scriptures:
Exodus 33:14
Matthew 28:20b
Psalm 121:7–8

Day 21

Gather Strength from God's Comfort

AS I THINK ABOUT THESE past two years with Daisy, I can't help but reflect on all that my family and I would have missed out on had we not opened our hearts to a new family dog. You read in the introduction how hard we all took the passing of our previous dog, Buddy. It would have been easy to stay in that place of loss. Most pet owners agree that their furry pals are members of the family. They are friends, confidants, mealtime participants, workout buddies, adventure companions, and much more. Their passing leaves a void, and the loss is very real. When our girls first mentioned getting a new dog, I was not ready. Thoughts of Buddy still brought sadness and tears as I vividly recalled his passing on our kitchen floor. But time passed, and the more the topic was approached, the softer my heart became toward the possibility. God was at work. In His sovereignty, He already knew He would bring Daisy into our lives, and He already knew what an impact she would have. We needed her. And her presence aided in healing our Buddy loss. Now I can smile as I think of Buddy, and we revisit memories that just make us laugh. We all agree that he would have just loved Daisy! Romans 8:28 tells us that God works all things for good for those who love Him and are called to His purpose. He took my sadness and gave me smiles—in the form of an absolutely wild, endlessly quirky, adorably loving golden-curled poodle.

Like you, I know many who have lost immediate family members and dear friends. Loss can leave us brokenhearted and in a place of sorrow that sometimes even time doesn't alleviate. God understands loss. Jesus set aside His throne to come to earth to save humanity, and God the Father lost His Son's heavenly presence. Jesus lost daily interaction with His family members when He entered public ministry to travel and teach all who would listen about the kingdom of Heaven. Jesus lost his closest friends when He was arrested the night before His death. He lost His dignity as He was stripped of His clothes and beaten beyond recognition. And as Jesus hung on the cross, for the first time ever He and His heavenly Father lost communion with one another as Jesus took the sin of the world upon Himself. Yes, God understands loss, the void it creates, and the intense sorrow that can follow. That is why, because of His personal experiences, Jesus understands our situations and our hearts better than anyone (Hebrews 4:15). He knows our pains and struggles. We do not have to pretend with Him, and when we lack the energy and transparency it takes to verbalize what lies within, we can just sit with Him, knowing He hears our thoughts and sees our hearts (Psalm 139:2, 44:21). No words required. He will meet us right where we are and for however long we are there.

Now it is wonderful to have family, friends, pastors, and godly counselors to come alongside us and share our burdens (Galatians 6:2). When we are ready, we can ask God to bring into our lives people we can trust and with whom we can share our hurts. They are a vital part of recovery, and God can, and does, use them to turn our sorrow into smiles. We don't always know why our loved ones pass, when they will pass, and the circumstances by which they pass. This knowledge is reserved for our Sovereign God alone. But the Bible assures us that He alone can change our mourning into rejoicing. This will ultimately be achieved when Jesus returns, and pain, sadness, and loss are no more. We all look forward to that glorious day! But until then, we can still turn to God each moment and lean on His ability to work all things for good. He can surround us with His loving arms and restore our joy for the day. It might be in unexpected ways, but He is faithful to do it.

Father above, we praise You that You know all that
we go through. You know our hurts, our sadness, our
loss. We thank You, Jesus, for your tender compassion
toward us and for how personally You can relate
to all that we go through here on earth. Help us
turn to You, knowing You heal the brokenhearted
and see and understand all that is within us. Lift
us up, Lord. In Your Name we pray, *amen.*

Key scriptures:
Isaiah 61:1–3
John 11:35
Psalm 34:18
1 Peter 5:7
Psalm 30:11–12
Nehemiah 8:10

Day 30

Receive God's Salvation Offer

VALUED READER, TODAY WE BEGIN our last devotional. I have loved sharing these stories of how my family and I have sensed God's presence and learned many lessons from Him through our wonderful new dog, Daisy. Many of you might relate to the lessons contained within these daily reads, having felt similar impressions from our amazing God who can use anything and anyone (yes, even our adorable pets) to bring about a scriptural truth or a moment of personal growth. But perhaps to some these reflections of God's presence in simple, everyday moments seem odd. Perhaps you do not know Jesus in this intimate way yet. I didn't always know Jesus this way either. I knew about Him my entire life, but I didn't really get to know Him until sixteen years ago. A faithful husband and a dear friend repeatedly shared about Jesus with me, and one spring day I had my own intimate moment with God that made His biblical truths come alive in my heart. I knew I needed to learn more, so I started reading the Bible every day and asked many questions. I always knew that Jesus was God's Son, sent to die for the sins of the world, but my relationship with Him wasn't personal. I thought that if I was a "good" enough person, I would go to Heaven when I died, and it didn't really affect my life too much more than that. But as I read the Bible and sought truth, God showed me that Jesus is very personal. He did not just come to die for the sins of the world; He came to die for *my* sins, me personally. The Ten Commandments (Deuteronomy 5), God's moral law, showed me how sinful I was. It is important to recognize our sin, so let's look at a few of these commandments. If we are honest with ourselves, we will admit that we have all lied, stolen (taken anything without permission regardless of the value), used God's name in vain, disobeyed our parents, murdered (gossip is murdering one's character), and committed adultery (Jesus teaches that looking at another with lust in the heart is the same as committing adultery). And this is only six of the ten commandments. I knew I was guilty of breaking God's moral law and as a result could never enter Heaven on my own merit because the payment for sin equals death (Romans 6:23). I needed a Savior!

Romans 3:23 tells us that *all* have sinned and fallen short of the glory of God. This means that none of us are good enough, and we can never "do" enough to enter God's holy presence. Even one "little white lie" separates us from Him because He cannot be in the presence of sin. So Jesus stepped in. He left Heaven and came to earth to close the gap between us and God by taking our sin punishment for us. Jesus is the Savior who, although sinless, willingly went to the cross and died in our place so that we may receive eternal life in Heaven. Because of Jesus, I now have a personal relationship with my heavenly Father, who no longer sees my sin but rather sees Jesus's sacrifice on my behalf. I don't need to be perfect because Jesus is perfect for me, and through Him I have everlasting life.

If you do not know Jesus as Savior, the good news is that today is a wonderful day for salvation (2 Corinthians 6:2). God so loved you, dear reader, that He sent His one and only Son, that whoever believes in Him shall not perish but have eternal life (John 3:16). When we accept His death as our sin payment and choose Him as our Savior, we are saved by faith and become children of God. By God's grace we are saved, through faith in Jesus. This is not something we can earn, but rather it is a gift (Ephesians 2:8–9). And when we receive this gift, we are made new, as we discussed on day 19. Jesus then sends His Holy Spirit to live within us to give us the wisdom and strength to follow Him each day. If you recognize your sin and want to turn away from it and receive Jesus as your Lord and Savior, pray the following prayer from your heart:

> Heavenly Father, You are a holy God who made
> a way for me to draw near to You and be with
> You forever. I recognize my sin before You, and
> I am sorry. I ask that You please forgive my sins
> and help me turn from them. I believe Jesus died
> on my behalf, and I ask Him into my life as my
> personal Savior. Teach me to follow You and to
> live for You. I ask in Jesus's holy Name, *amen.*

If this is the day of salvation for you, congratulations! Welcome into the family of God! Read the Bible every day to grow in God's truths and follow Jesus's teachings. I also encourage new believers to join a Bible-teaching Christian church for support and fellowship. And pray to God on all occasions with all kinds of prayers and requests (day 4). Pray for growth, strength, ears to hear His Spirit within you, and for Him to show you how to live for Him. I might never know you or whether you accepted Jesus as Savior because of this devotional, but I will be saying these prayers in faith, knowing our heavenly Father sees exactly who these prayers are intended for. May God bless you and keep you and continue to grow all our hearts in love and gratitude for His indescribable gift of Savior Jesus!